Dear Humanity

Marie-Josée Thibault

30 Messages From the Blessed Virgin Mary Spoken During Advent 2021

BOOK 2

Dear Humanity : Book 2
30 Messages From the Blessed Virgin Mary
Spoken During Advent 2021

Published by Abba Books LLC
abbabooksllc@gmail.com
Copyright © 2023 Marie-Josée Thibault

All Rights Reserved

No part of this publication may be reproduced, distributed, or transmitted i
any form or by any means, including photocopying, recording, or other
electronic or mechanical methods, without the prior written permission of
the publisher.

1st Edition, 2023
Designed and Edited by Abba Books LLC
ISBN: 979-8-9875984-4-3

Abba Books LLC
34972 Newark Blvd, #441
Newark, CA 94560
www.abbamyfatheriloveyou.com
https://www.facebook.com/AbbaILoveYouBooks/

Thy Peace on Earth must be achieved.

No light, no litany must be spared to honor Thy Grace.

-Saint Paul

CONTENT

PREFACE	VI		
The Season of Advent	1	The transcendance	27
Glorious Return	5	annunciation	31
My Presence	7	Elizabeth and I	35
My Mantle	11	The Supernatural Birth of	
Act of Contrition	13	Jesus	37
Events on Your Doorstep	17	Angels	41
God the Father Almighty	21	Saint Joseph	45
Your Purification	25	Saint John the Baptist	47

My return	51	Light of Christ	79
Your Holy Mary	53	Light of Christ	83
Reconciliation	57	The End Times	87
You and Me	61	My Love	89
My Mantle of Blue Suns	63	The Night	93
my love	67	The Father	95
the rosary	71	The Father	99
Your Advocate	75	About The Author	104

PREFACE

Dictated by the Virgin Mary

My friends on Earth, I appeared to Marie-Josée at the command of God who ordained me. Marie-Josée is my unique and special spiritual daughter and I visit her daily after the evening meal. I love her so much! She and I have come together miraculously through the years, but especially through this miraculous book that you hold in your hands.

Ask God that I may visit you in the same way as Marie-Josée, and, thanks to my intercession, the infinitely good Father will grant it to you! Amen!

Written by the author

I love, I adore, I venerate, the Beautiful and Holy Virgin Mary who visits me daily! My heart leaps with joy when I see her materialize before my eyes! She often smiles. She is sad sometimes. She cries at times. She is so expressive! I love her so much!

I especially like the way we both pray to God the Father and the way she articulates her prayer in my presence. She speaks to God clearly and directly, with adoration and humility, while being firm and

Dear Humanity

detailed. I learn so much by her side! I love her so much!

Hail, Mary, full of grace,

the Lord is with thee.

Blessed art thou amongst women

and blessed is the fruit of thy womb, Jesus.

Holy Mary, Mother of God,

pray for us sinners,

now and at the hour of our death. Amen.

Marie-Josée Thibault

FREE DOWNLOAD

Get your free copy of :
"Saint Padre Pio Speaks: Book 1"
when you sign up to the
author's VIP mailing list!
Get started here:

www.abbamyfatheriloveyou.com

1

THE SEASON OF ADVENT

Dear humanity:

My children, my dear ones, my adorable ones, open your hearts very widely for the marvelous messages that I am announcing to you today! The season of Advent, my dear ones, prepares for the coming of Christ the King unto your hearts and the coming of His Beloved Mother, who is also your Divine

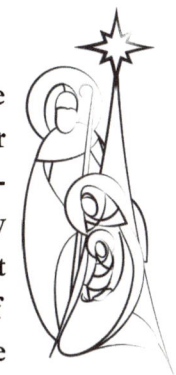

Mother, the Virgin Mary! Amen!

My loves, my children of Love, do not be deceived by the social pressure to engage in the festivities of Christmas that emphasize exaggerated commercial consumption, specially regarding the spiritual teaching of your own children.

Rejoicing is welcome, of course, but one should focus on the closeness and adoration of Jesus and everything that He is for the human race. Jesus is our Savior! Our Lord! Our King! Our Master! Our Light! Our Divine Mercy! Our Redeemer! Our Lamb of God! Our Life! Our Sacred Heart! Our Paradise! Our Christ! Our Eucharist! Our Son of God! My Beloved Son! Our God! Our Love! Our Glory! And above all, Our Baby Jesus of Love, born in the manger of love! Amen!

Come into my loving arms each and every one of you, dear children of the miracle of Love that is your birth in the heavenly worlds that await you! I love you. Amen!

Dear Humanity

2

GLORIOUS RETURN

Dear humanity:

The season of Advent, my loves, is the preparation for the actual birth of Jesus in your heart at Christmas and a preparation for His glorious return to the whole Earth in a glorious light so intense that planet Earth will tremble with joy... and terror... with joy for the disciples of

Marie-Josée Thibault

His Sacred Heart, united with my Sacred Heart, but also, unfortunately, terror is for those who refused the multiple invitations that God the Father granted to you all.

Discern, my friends, my loves, the Love of the Eternal Father for you through Jesus, my Mighty Son, and Myself, your Mother in Heaven!

I bless you, and I love you.

Dear Humanity

3

MY PRESENCE

Dear humanity:

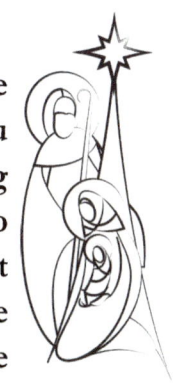

My children of love, awaken to the love that God bestows upon you every day of your life. I am not referring to the riches of this falling world but to the wealth of the Catholic religion! It teaches you the truth of my presence among you in your heart, as well as the presence of all the Saints in Paradise, the Angels of God, and the pure souls in Paradise, who pray for you constantly day and night!

On your behalf, I say thank you to our Glorious Father, Abba Father, our Creator, and our God! Amen! I ask you to make your profession of faith with me. Say it with me, Mother and child reunited:

We believe in one God, the Father Almighty, Maker of Heaven and Earth, of all things visible and invisible.

We believe in one Lord, Jesus Christ, the only begotten Son of God, born of the Father before all ages. God from God, Light from Light, true God from true God, begotten, not made, consubstantial with the Father; through Him, all things were made. For us men

Dear Humanity: Book 1

and for our salvation, He came down from Heaven, and by the Holy Spirit was incarnate of the Virgin Mary and became man. For our sake, He was crucified under Pontius Pilate, He suffered death and was buried and rose again on the third day in accordance with the Scriptures. He ascended into Heaven and is seated at the right hand of the Father. He will come again in glory to judge the living and the dead, and His Kingdom will have no end.

We believe in the Holy Spirit, the Lord, the giver of life, who proceeds from the Father and the Son, who, with the Father and the Son, is adored and glorified, who has spoken through the prophets. We believe in One, Holy, Catholic and Apostolic Church. We confess one baptism for the forgiveness of sins, and we look forward to the resurrection of the dead and the life of the world to come. Amen.

THE BIRTH OF *Christ*

Dear Humanity

4

MY MANTLE

Dear humanity:

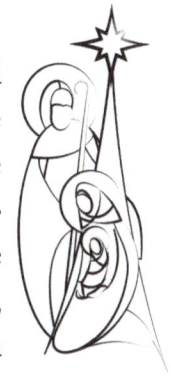

My children, my loves, remain well hidden under my mantle of blue suns, a unique, solid, and certain refuge before the forces of evil that are multiplying on Earth and that will become more and more visible in your streets, in your establishments, and in your own homes. I love you, I protect you, and I hide you from the enemy.

Satan, my dears, really exists, and he has recruited an army of demons that roam the Earth, as the prayer of Saint Michael indicates.

The purity that is mine, my Immaculate Heart, my Immaculate Conception, my Immaculate Whiteness, institutes an extraordinary and invincible weapon against the forces of evil. And this, Satan knows.

When you live a true relationship with me, with your Divine and intimate Mother, your Virgin Mary, Satan cannot approach you. My purity is like a blaze of fire that destroys all evil forces. Such is the extraordinary Divine Grace that God has bestowed upon me: I, His humble servant.

May God be blessed for showing so much mercy unto you, my beloved children!

Amen!

5

ACT OF CONTRITION

Dear humanity:

My very great children, my very great loves, I ask you today to make a sincere and general act of contrition regarding the insolences, blasphemies, and infamies that you have perpetrated against my Immaculate Heart during your lifetime. For my pure heart does not

tolerate any defilement of any of my children.

Say this: My beloved Divine Mother, my Mother in Heaven, I ask you to forgive me all my sins committed against you, dear beloved Divine Mother, dear Mother in Heaven, dear all-pure Mother, true Immaculate Heart, and never again repeat them. Amen. Alleluia!

For I am the Mother of Mercy, the Mother of the forgiveness that God grants you through me and thanks to me. I love you!

My power in the eyes of God to bring you inner well-being and to proceed to the purification of your souls is far greater than you can imagine.

I love you so much.

Amen!

6

EVENTS ON YOUR DOORSTEP

Dear humanity:

My little children, the atrocious events on your doorstep include natural cataclysms, military crises, plagues of disease and pestilence, and economic disasters, in addition to food supply difficulties far beyond the most serious and severe scenarios you can imagine.

Marie-Josée Thibault

This is part of the Great Plan for the Salvation of Humankind conceived by God the Father. Be vigilant, pray, and remain well under the protection of my mantle of blue suns, for tribulations are at your doorstep.

Your protection is ensured through your faith in me, your Divine and Personal Mother, your very powerful Mother in Heaven, your Virgin Mary; in Jesus, my Beloved Son, God the Son, the commander of God's Army; in the Saints in Paradise who surround you and who love you; in the legions of Angels who move across the Earth for your blessing; and above all, through your faith in God the Father Almighty, who loves you so much and will grant you His Divine Mercy. Pray. I love you.

Let us give glory to God, Our Almighty, Heavenly Father, Our Creator, and Our Judge. Amen! Alleluia!

Dear Humanity

7

GOD THE FATHER ALMIGHTY

Dear humanity:

My little children of the Earth, listen to me carefully. The birth, the life, the love abided, and the death of every human being who walks on Earth are determined by God alone. He is the Supreme Governor of your life, no matter how much faith you have in Him—

Marie-Josée Thibault

or in Jesus or in me. God, the Almighty Father, is the Supreme Governor of all His Creation and all His creatures in all the kingdoms that you know: human, animal, plant, mineral. The Father decides all things, at all times, and in all places, in relation to all His creatures of His Creation, for all His creatures are born from His Own Hands and possess His Breath of Life.

Alleluia! Let us give thanks to God, who loves you all as a Father, and who has already prepared your salvation, each and every one of you! Amen!

Prostrate yourselves, therefore, before the Power, the Supremacy, the Justice, but above all, the Mercy of our God—Love, God our Eternal Father, Our Creator to all. Amen! Alleluia!

Dear Humanity

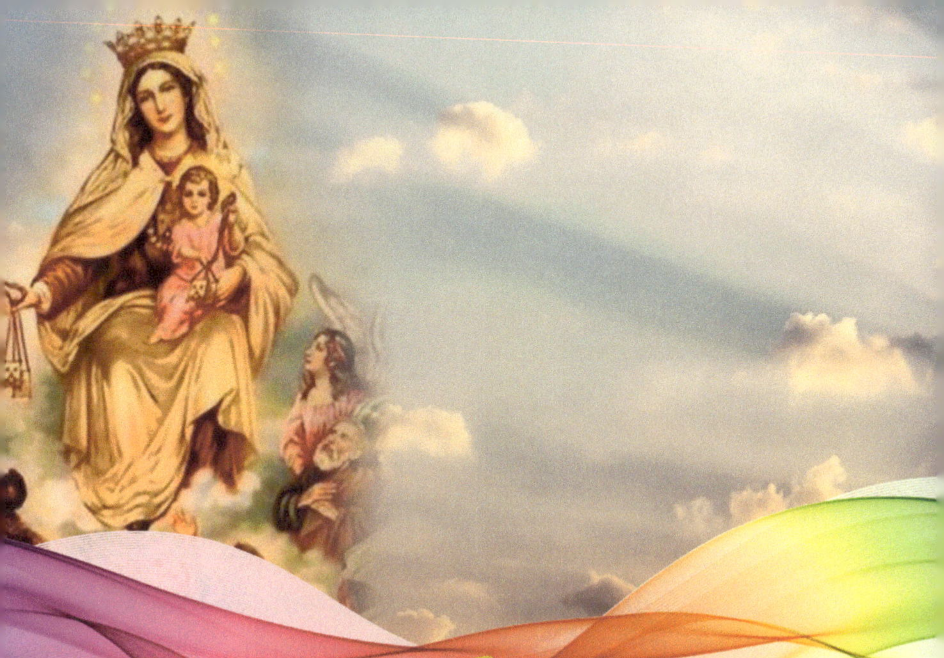

8

YOUR PURIFICATION

Dear humanity:

My friends, my beloved, look in a mirror. What do you see? Skin on the surface, your eyes, your nose, your mouth, your hair, your body... Do you see your soul? No, you might say. However, I, the Virgin Mary, your Divine and personal Mother, see it. I see your souls perfectly

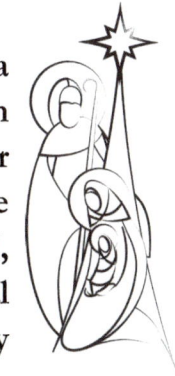

well, each and every one of you, and I see in perfect light the filth that stains your souls.

Allow me, my dears, my loves, to thoroughly cleanse your souls, to purify you, to make you white as snow, to transform you into a Christ like Jesus, my Son and my God. I love you.

My Immaculate Whiteness, my dears, is an extraordinary grace given to me by the Eternal Father, our Creator to all. It allows me, the Virgin Mary, the Blessed Mother, your Divine and Unique Mother, to protect you from Satan in a supernatural way in dimensions of the universe that you do not suspect. For Satan cannot come near me... Satan coming near me would mean his permanent destruction, and this he knows.

Alleluia! Let us give thanks to God, Our Eternal Father, for allowing you to read these lines of love from your Mother in Heaven and allowing me to purify you and make you little by little immaculate and therefore invincible before Satan!

Amen!

Dear Humanity

9

THE TRANSCENDANCE

Dear humanity:

My children, my loves, listen to me carefully. Life on Earth, my beloved children, is strewn with trials and tribulations according to the Divine Plan of Life that God laid out in advance for each and every one of you. The saints in Paradise, the Angels of God, the pure

souls, Jesus, and I, the Most Holy Virgin Mary, guide you, protect you, console you, and above all, we desire at the highest point your glorious entry into Paradise following the passage that is death.

Pray, my children. Pray, and you will be saved by Divine Mercy unto your soul! Amen!

By virtue of the transcendence of the visible worlds that enable communication between us, I speak to you from here above, from Paradise, and I speak to you from here below, in your heart.

Be assured, my loves, my children of love, that my presence in you, around you, and through you is true, real, eternal, and merciful, as is that of my Beloved Son, Jesus of Nazareth, Son of God, Our Lord and Our God, and the Apostle Saint Paul, the apostle of conversion to Christ Jesus, our everything! Amen!

Alleluia! Alleluia! Alleluia! Glory to God for this miraculous teaching, source of hope, and instrument of understanding of the wonderful mysteries of the universe! Am

Dear Humanity

10

ANNUNCIATION

Dear humanity:

My children of my heart, listen to me well. Today, I recount to you the miraculous event of the Annunciation. The Angel Gabriel appeared in the family home where I lived with my parents while they were away.

One evening, during my daily prayer, I found myself in an abnormal trance, such as I had never experienced before. I felt alert and sleepy at the same time. Suddenly, I perceived a celestial, friendly presence near me, a little apart. I continued my prayer. The angelic form became denser, brighter, more benevolent, and above all, closer to me. I was amazed!

The Angel Gabriel spoke with me much longer and much more elaborately than the Catholic religion teaches you. Of course, how would you know without my detailed testimony?

The Angel Gabriel came to visit me several times during my pregnancy. His education, his precise instructions, and above all, his angelic protection were indispensable to the normal, albeit supernatural, course of my pregnancy. I love you.

Let us give glory to God: Eternal Father, we pray to You, we adore You, we give You thanks for so much beauty, for so much goodness, for so much love, and for so much mercy. Amen!

Dear Humanity

11

ELIZABETH AND I

Dear humanity:

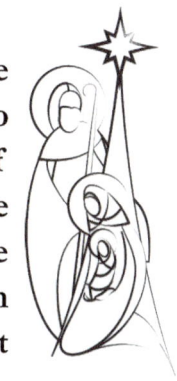

My friends, my loves, **God the Father** asked me personally to visit my cousin Elizabeth, the mother of Saint John the Baptist, shortly after the conception of Jesus in my womb. The cosmic presence of God, Jesus, within me allowed me to be in a transcendent relationship with the Father in an infinitely elevated vibrational manner.

The Holiness of Jesus, Son of God, spread throughout me and allowed my swift and unparalleled sanctification on Earth.

My visit to Elizabeth's home, therefore, took place with sentiments of ineffable joy and hope.

Elizabeth and I became extra-sensitive souls and very close to each other, blessed by the Father.

I thank the Father Creator for this miracle today! Such Love! Such Power! Such Mercy!

I love you.

Dear Humanity

12

SUPERNATURAL BIRTH OF JESUS

Dear humanity:

The nativity of my Glorious Son more than 2,000 years ago, which you celebrate on beautiful Christmas Day, was a miraculous cosmic moment unprecedented on Earth. The Angels of God assisted me in an unimaginable, albeit delicate way, and thus the birth of Jesus

Marie-Josée Thibault

took place in a supernatural manner, without any pain for me.

Divine Providence was manifested through me precisely according to God's plan for the birth of Jesus on Earth, God made man for me, for you, for the whole of creation.

Let us give glory to my Son Jesus Christ, our Lord and our God, for so much divine mercy! Alleluia!

I desire, my beloved child, to see in your soul a doubtless and total trust in the absolute truth of this miraculous fact: the supernatural birth of Jesus, our King.

I use this trust in me, your beloved Mother, Holy Mary, in my words of divine origin to amplify it, to bless it, and more importantly, to offer it to God the Almighty Father to facilitate your glorious entry into Paradise at the time of the passage that is death.

Blessed are my sons and daughters who obey my commandments, for the Paradise where we live is theirs! Amen! Alleluia!

Dear Humanity

13

ANGELS

Dear humanity:

My children of the Earth, listen to me well. Herod's martyrs, the newborns and children under age two, did indeed happen—a tragedy beyond compare. I experienced with Joseph and Jesus appalling moments that were inexpressible for a young family like ours.

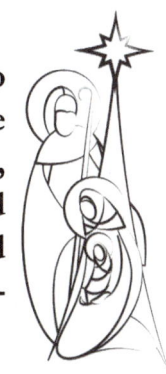

Glory to God! The Angels of God visited us and educated us regarding our extraordinary mystical mission for the rest of history and for all humanity. Friendly Angels also educated my young Jesus in a special way and spent many hours with Him during His childhood.

Saint Joseph and I were fascinated by Jesus' unheard-of talents of learning and behaving supremely wisely, and by His natural love and care for others. Jesus was the perfect child for me: His Mother, Holy Mary, and His father, Saint Joseph. I love you.

Come, my children. Come into my arms and let us pray together to our Lord Jesus Christ, our King and our everything, my glorious Son, and the Son of God! Amen!

Dear Humanity

Dear Humanity

14

SAINT JOSEPH

Dear humanity:

My friends, my children, my loves, listen to me well. My husband on Earth, Saint Joseph, was a generous, devoted, and very pious man, and above all, he was an observant of the Jewish religion. His love for me, the Most Blessed Virgin Mary, and for Jesus, our child in the eyes of society, was immense and unconditional.

The Angels guided him several times during my pregnancy, during the perinatal and infantile period and the youth of our Child in Egypt, and during our return to Galilee in Nazareth.

Saint Joseph is a very great Saint in Paradise to whom you should dedicate yourself in the same manner as to me. Honor and glory are due to Saint Joseph! Pray to Saint Joseph very often. I love you.

Alleluia! Alleluia! Alleluia! I give glory to our Father Creator for enabling us to meet today, Mother and Child, with Jesus and Joseph, an event of Love lived through the Holy and Eternal Family, celebrated with joy by all the inhabitants of Paradise!

Amen!

Dear Humanity

15

SAINT JOHN THE BAPTIST

Dear humanity:

Saint John the Baptist and Jesus became close childhood friends because of their familial closeness and similar age. The details of their unique mission eluded them at a young age, and their desires to play like young children were judicious and understandable!

Marie-Josée Thibault

Therefore, Jesus and John were very close friends. Elizabeth and I witnessed in them an astounding wisdom and frank, upright kindness toward others in their daily lives.

Let us give glory to God for His plan of salvation for humankind, which included a normal and happy childhood lived and shared between Jesus and John! Amen!

Alleluia! Alleluia! Alleluia! Let us give glory to God, who loves you and who has already prepared the salvation of your soul through Jesus and John! Amen!

Dear Humanity

16

MY RETURN

Dear humanity:

Dear children, my children, prepare for my return to Earth! Just as my glorious Son will return among you in a cosmic coronation of an absolute and sovereign Power that will shake the whole of Creation, I will be there by His side, in grace and glory!

Marie-Josée Thibault

I thank my Creator and my God, Our Heavenly Father, for so many blessings on me, His humble servant. For behold, henceforth, all generations will call me blessed (Luke 1:48).

For my Beloved Son, Son of God, Jesus of Nazareth, is united with me, and this in all dimensions of the universe. For I, the Divine Mother, and Jesus, the Divine Son, are indivisible: I in Him, and He in me. We are one Heart-Love, one Heart-Servant of the Eternal Father, Abba Father. Amen! Glory to God in the Highest Heaven!

Dear Humanity

17

YOUR HOLY MARY

Dear humanity:

My children, do not be saddened by the events that are fast approaching. Stay close to me, very close to your Divine Mother, your beloved Mother. Pray your rosary every day, follow the ordinances of the Catholic Church, keep a beautiful statue of me near your bed, and know that I behold you and love you passionately as a good mother to all of her children.

Understand this day, dear child of Love, that I reside both in Heaven and in your heart, my little one. I capture and share with you all the events in your life, big and small, from second to second, day to day, year to year—and eternally—and I perfectly capture the infinitesimal nuances of every emotion, every thought, every word, every gesture, every work that unfolds in your soul and your life.

Dear Humanity: Book 1

I cry with you when you cry. I rejoice in your successes. I encourage you when adversities accumulate.

For I am the Divine Mother of every soul that populates the Earth, and this intimately, lovingly, uniquely, and eternally.

I am your Divine Mother, I am your Virgin Mary, I am your Holy Mary, I am your Mother in Heaven. I love you.

RECONCILIATION

Dear humanity:

My friends, my sweet children, listen to me well since I am the Virgin Mary, Mother of our beloved Jesus, Savior to all. Today, my dear child, I desire that you make an act of contrition during the sacrament of reconciliation with the priest of your choice, or at least that you

initiate this process today. This is very important for the salvation of your soul. Regardless of the difficulties inherent in the fulfillment of this sacrament, I will personally help you achieve it.

I repeat: I want you to contact a priest today to confess. I will be there with you during your confession, and I will inspire you. I love you, my child of joy.

The end times are near. Be ready at all levels; do not delay prayers any longer. Now is God's chosen moment for your redemption through Jesus and Mary! Amen!

Dear Humanity

19

YOU AND ME

Dear humanity:

My child, my joy, my reason for being on Earth, it is your unique, personal, and intimate Mother who speaks to you today, your own Virgin Mary, your own Divine Mother, your instrument of co-redemption with Jesus, my wonderful Son, your agent of Mercy before God, and

my Son Jesus.

The prayers said together, you and I united, touch the Heart of the Father in a very special way, and there is no request that can be refused to me. Trust in me, your Blessed Mother, both in Heaven and on Earth, in your heart. I love you.

My presence in your life through these words that you are reading at this very moment, my child of Love, is truly miraculous. Pray your rosary with joy and peace daily. I will be close to you at the moment of your agony and the passage that is death. I promise you that today. I love you.

Dear Humanity

20

MY MANTLE OF BLUE SUNS

Dear humanity:

My dear, the consecration of your soul to me, the Most Blessed Virgin Mary, to my mantle of blue suns, is important, and I invite you to consecrate yourself today.

Repeat after me: Holy Mary, my good

Mother, my sweet Virgin Mary, I ask you today to accept my soul under your mantle of blue suns, refuge and shelter of Catholics during the events and torments to come, and never to allow me to let my soul drift away from it.

Mother of Love, I really love you, and I belong to you. Keep me close to you and sheltered under your all-blue and all-powerful mantle, for there is the sun that annihilates Satan as a secret weapon.

My Mother in Heaven, Holy Mary, I love you. Amen!

In the Name of the Father, and of the Son, and of the Holy Spirit. Amen!

Dear Humanity

21

MY LOVE

Dear humanity:

My loves, I want to tell you today of the greatness of my Love! My Love is vaster than the entire universe, exceeds the three dimensions where you live, cannot be qualified or quantified in any way, and cannot be contained or described by any book on Earth!

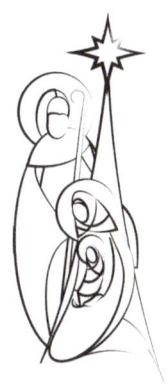

Dear Humanity: Book 1

My Love for you, my child of Love, originates and manifests its plentitude in the very Heart of Abba Father, our Heavenly Father and Creator!

My Love for you will never end since your soul, my dear, is in my hands for eternity!

How much I love you! Your Virgin Mary, your beautiful Divine Mother who adores you. Amen!

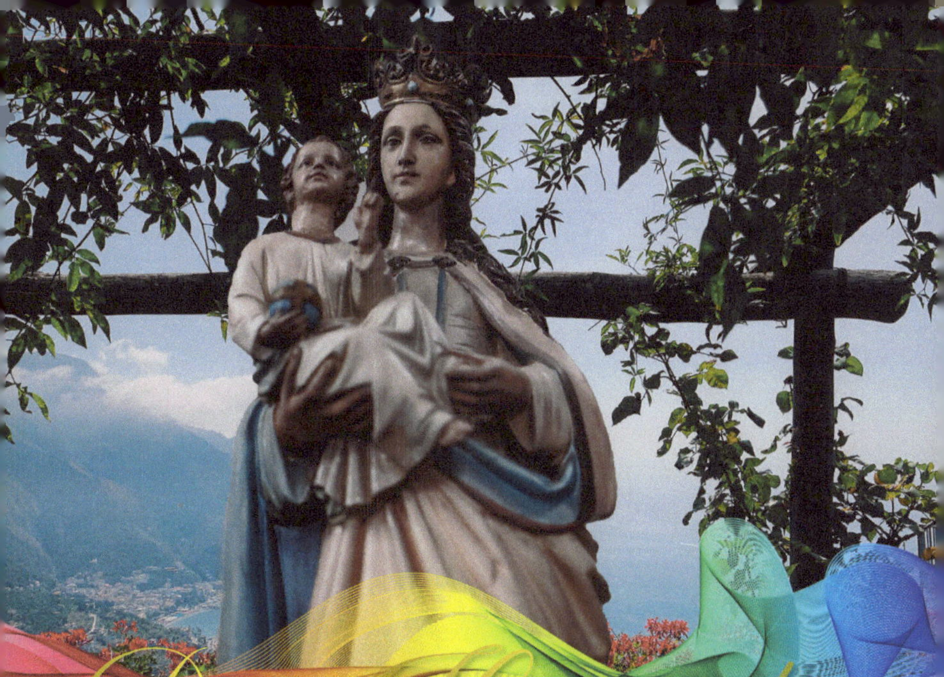

Dear Humanity

22

THE ROSARY

Dear humanity:

My friends, my loves, listen to me. The recitation of the rosary, my children, is a fundamental prayer practice in the life of every Catholic throughout the world. Try to set aside this 30-minute spiritual union with me and Jesus, not only for mercy in the acute events of

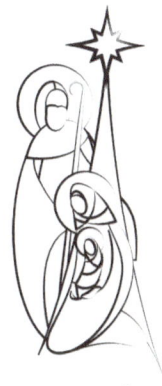

your life, but also, above all, to prepare a peaceful and serene death in my miraculous presence.

Pray your rosary as early as possible during the day to modify and elevate the state of your soul for the rest of the day. I love you!

Know also, my child, that the rosary in your hands has a sublime magnetism that reverberates in all dimensions of the universe. A single rosary has a dazzling light seen from here, from Paradise! The glorious brilliance of a rosary pierces the heavy and low dimensions of the Earth's surface with an ineffable bluish and magnificent illumination that makes me tremble with joy!

Dear Humanity: Book 1

Oh, if you only knew the power of one rosary in the Heart of the Eternal Father! You would never fail to recite it with delight and faith! Amen!

Dear Humanity

23

YOUR ADVOCATE

Dear humanity:

Dear children of Love, I desire that today you understand an essential element of my teaching included in this holy book. My power of intercession before God is more vigorous and unique than you can imagine; however, understand, my children, that I have no power

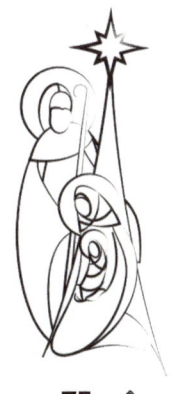

over the decisions in your life.

In other words, my power consists specifically of prayer and intercession, which touches the Heart of the Father in a very special way. However, I cannot ordain or govern your life. I am your advocate, not your judge. This clarification is needed today.

God—God the Father, God the Son in the Highest, God the Holy Spirit—One in the Holy Trinity, governs you supremely and exclusively, and makes all decisions in your lives.

What is your petition? A new job? The cure of a serious illness? The return of a lost family member?

Imagine a bridge that extends to the wounded feet of Jesus. That bridge is your faith and your journey that brings you to His feet! Jesus stretches out His arms to you. He wishes to grant you the desired grace.

I, your Divine Mother, your Virgin Mary, I accompany you, I guide your steps, I inspire you, I motivate you, I make you strong, I cover you with my mantle of blue suns. We progress together on the bridge to the desired grace, to Jesus, to Grace Himself, your Savior, the Word made flesh, my Glorious Son! The Angels and Saints in Paradise also support and guide you.

And God the Father Almighty absorbs everything: our petitions, our faith, our prayers, our devotions, our intercession, our love. Do you see?

I am prostrated before the throne of God, and I pray with tears in supplication on your behalf for the petition requested: This is my role as Divine Mother toward all my children. I will pray for you, my child, during your life, your agony, your death, and, if necessary, after your death. I can inspire you, guide you, support you, console you, and, above all, protect you from Satan. This is the special ministry that the Father has bestowed upon me.

Never stop praying to me, for my prayers destined for the Father are uniquely powerful, and never stop praying to God directly, our Eternal Father Creator, who loves His children much more than you can imagine! Amen!

Dear Humanity

24

LIGHT OF CHRIST

Dear humanity:

My great loves, listen to me carefully. I am explaining to you today the mystery of my multiple apparitions under different mystical manifestations and with well-identified spiritual goals.

The etheric dimensions, my dears,

consist of extremely high vibrational waves that you cannot comprehend. The Universal Mother, the Universal Lady, is occasionally entrusted with a specific mission ordained by God the Father according to social, political, and catastrophic events on Earth.

The Universal Mother has abided in the Heart of the Father since the very beginning of Genesis. The Universal Mother was conceived at the same time as Jesus, Her Wonderful Son, at the time of Genesis.

The Universal Mother, therefore, materialized in me, the Virgin Mary, the Mother of our Savior, your First Lady, 2,000 years ago.

For 2,000 years, the Universal Mother has materialized into several ladies and has assumed varied and planned feminine human characteristics that are always sweet and beautiful: Our Lady of Lourdes, Our Lady of Fatima, Our Lady of Guadalupe, Our Lady of Medjugorje, Our Lady of La Salette, and so on.

The Universal Mother, Your Universal Lady, responds immediately and creatively to the commands of God the Father to bestow mercy on Earth through these Marian apparitions. I thank God for so much mercy on Earth! Amen! I love you.

Dear Humanity

25

LIGHT OF CHRIST

Dear humanity:

My friends, my loves, my children, life on Earth is filled with adventures, adversity, and especially mistakes on your part. The mistakes are committed on several levels: your actions, your thoughts, your emotions, and your decisions, and these from second to second,

minute to minute, day to day, and so on.

Why go adrift? Why regret these small and big decisions that sometimes generate so much suffering? Why are you moving away from your own inner life?

Verily, verily, I say unto you, every act, thought, emotion, and decision is made either in the Light of Christ united to me, the sweet Virgin Mary, your Mother in Heaven, or outside the Light of Christ, and outside of me. See?

Keep your two feet solid,

Dear Humanity: Book 1

well anchored, and well rooted in Jesus, my Glorious Son, and in me, your Divine Mother, your Lady, your Virgin Mary, at all times. Listen! Pray! Meditate!

I give glory to God to allow me to teach you this fundamental truth today! Amen!

Dear Humanity

26

THE END TIMES

Dear humanity:

My friends, my loves, my children, it is very important that you listen to me today. My children, the End Times have arrived.

I have already said so, and I will repeat it unto you again: The End Times have

arrived. I ask you today, my dearest child, whom I adore and to whom I am speaking at this day and at this hour, to have a powerful and decisive shock of conscience regarding the truth of my words and the urgency that I convey to you.

Do not delay any longer! From this moment on, you must be effectively and totally converted into Christ Jesus and proclaim Him God, Lord, and Redeemer, at this very moment when you are reading these lines. Say it with me:

Yes! Jesus is my Lord!

Yes! Jesus is my God!

Yes! Jesus is my Savior!

Yes! Jesus, I love you! Amen!

O Mary, conceived without sin, pray for us who have recourse to you! Amen!

Dear Humanity

27

MY LOVE

Dear humanity:

My children, my loves, my children of Love, learn today the measure, the value, and the power of my Love! I was born in Heaven at the time of Genesis, and I have carried you in my womb since that glorious time! I waited patiently for this moment of reunion

Marie-Josée Thibault

between you and me, spiritual Mother and spiritual child, Mother of Jesus and child of Jesus, Mother of your heart and you, heart of my heart. Amen! Alleluia!

My Love has no earthly measure possible because my Love extends from one end to the other of the whole creation. The value of my Love for you, dear child, is known in the very Heart of God the Father, Creator of all.

The power of my Love overcomes the most difficult obstacles, brings miracles daily, and is expressed with all its fullness at the time of the passage that is death. For I facilitate your entry into Paradise, as promised by the rosary, dear children of my Heavenly Glory! Amen. Alleluia!

Dear Humanity

28

THE NIGHT

Dear humanity:

My dear children, my children of joy, listen to me well. Night is naturally reserved for sleep and rest. But, unfortunately, during the night, there is a fierce battle between the forces of evil and the forces of good outside your doors: on the street, in backyards, in open public estab-

lishments, and sometimes even in your own homes.

The Angels of God who protect and guard you are waging a constant fight against Satan and his demons who roam the Earth at all times, but especially at nightfall. Pray, my children, pray!

Do not delay returning home in the evening and avoid busy public establishments, especially where there is alcohol consumption, for the enemy is there in multitude. My children, my loves, stay well hidden under my mantle of blue suns. I love you.

Dear Humanity

29

THE FATHER

Dear humanity:

My children, my loves, dear precious children of the Father, listen to me well. Draw closer to the loving Father, for it is His most great goodness that frees you from your sins! Speak directly to the Father often, and share with Him all your love for Him!

Each of your lives on Earth, in fact, unfolds in the Heart of the Father, the God Creator of all life forms in His Creation! Be humble, be grateful, be in conversation, be in confession, be in relationship, be in union, be in trust, be His child, be one-on-one with Him, the Father, and above all, be in constant prayer.

The Lord's Prayer is the prayer of the Father, for He composed it Himself and transmitted it to His Son, my glorious Jesus of Nazareth, to teach it to all humanity. Therefore, pray often the Lord's Prayer, and in this, the Father will be pleased. I love you.

Glory to God, whose very great goodness frees you from your sins! Amen!

Dear Humanity

30

THE FATHER

Dear humanity:

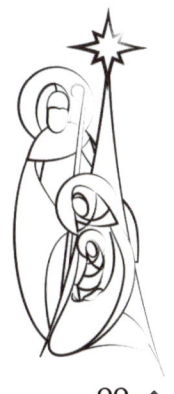

My most beautiful child, I thank you for these tender and unique moments between us, Mother and child, Virgin Mary and disciple of Jesus, sharing one sole reality of Love: the birth of my Jesus renewed at every moment between us. I gave birth to you the same way that I gave birth to my Savior, Jesus. Do you see?

What a beautiful miracle of Love! What a masterpiece of Love as conceived by Abba Father, who loves us all passionately!

Glory to God in the Highest Heaven for so much mercy toward His Creation!

I love you, and I will talk to you again very soon.

Stay in constant prayer.

Pray your rosary daily with Jesus and me.

The Virgin Mary,

Your Divine Mother

Dear Humanity

Dear Humanity: Book 1

AFTERWORD

Like the first book, Dear Humanity—Book 1, this publication contains a series of messages to the human race dictated to me by multiple apparitions of the Blessed Virgin Mary concerning the importance of prayer, the details of her life, her relationships to God the Father and to the Savior, Jesus Christ, the intercessory role that she plays in prayer, preparations that should be made for the End Times, and many other subjects that are of critical importance to the souls of her readers. This book will be very special amongst devout Catholics and, with Abba Father willing, an audience among humanity at large.

Blessed Virgin Mary, I love you so much!

Marie-Josée

ABOUT THE AUTHOR

Marie-Josée Thibault's life is in no way similar to yours. When she wakes, the saints of Heaven visit her, talk to her, teach her, and pray intensely with her. When such mystical sessions draw to a close, she greets with great respect and deep reverence the Masters of the Heavenly Court. This servant of the Lord spends the rest of the day in the company of her guardian angel, who continues her spiritual education and ceaselessly protects her from the perils of this fallen world.

Bestowed by the Heavenly Father, her gifts of clairvoyance and clairaudience allow her to remain in continuous contact with the supernatural dimension juxtaposed with ours, where the soul is born of the Spirit through Jesus and Mary. She prays that, one day soon, the entire human race will give glory to the Father, the Son, and the Holy Spirit.

Also by Marie-Josee Thibault

Dear Humanity: Book 1

Abba, Your Father, Speaks: Book I

Abba, Your Father, Speaks: Book II

Angel Gabriel Speaks: Book I

Saint Padre Pio Speaks: Book 1

Marie-Josée Thibault

FREE DOWNLOAD

Get your free copy of :
"Saint Padre Pio Speaks: Book 1"
when you sign up to the
author's VIP mailing list!
Get started here:

www.abbamyfatheriloveyou.com

www.ingramcontent.com/pod-product-compliance
Lightning Source LLC
Chambersburg PA
CBHW041609220426
43667CB00001B/16